W9-AON-709

Yale

A CELEBRATION

Yale

A CELEBRATION

Selected & Edited by
Alison E. Brody and J. Kenneth Brody

Illustrations by
Leslie Ansteth Colonna

Foreword by
Richard C. Levin

Old Ivy Press, LLC
Portland, Oregon

Selections and Foreword copyright © 2001
by Old Ivy Press, LLC, 1331 SW Broadway, Portland, Oregon 97201

Illustrations copyright © 2000 by Leslie Ansteth Colonna

ISBN 0-9673674-0-9

Printed in Hong Kong

IN LOVING MEMORY

Charles S. Brody
of the Yale College Class of 1916
and the Yale Law School Class of 1918

and
Lydia G. Brody, his wife

IN LASTING FRIENDSHIP

The Yale College Class of 1944

The Yale College Class of 1995

Note and Acknowledgments

THE DATES following the attributions for each selection are the dates of the historical document or, in the case of literary selections, the date of publication. The literary sources are contained in the index under the author's name. The watercolor illustrations are also fully indexed.

The black and white drawings have been chosen from the vast array of stone carvings, architectural details, and decorations that are found on the walls of University buildings. They are a tribute to the versatility of Leslie Ansteth Colonna, who has contributed the forty watercolor paintings that adorn this book.

We are profoundly grateful to Yale President Richard C. Levin, who has contributed a Foreword that truly introduces the reader to the spirit of the book, to Linda Koch Lorimer, Vice President and Secretary of the University and Secretary of the Tercentennial, and to Janet Lindner, Director of Tercentennial and Special Projects. Their interest and support have not only been vital to the success of this book project, but have also added greatly to the pleasure of creating it.

From concept to publication, the encyclopedic knowledge and wise counsel of Richard Abel, Portland's internationally known bookman and book trade counselor, have made this book a reality.

Sandra J. Brody, Yale '16 daughter-in-law, '44 wife, and '95 mother, has lent her helping hand and enthusiastic support to every stage of this book.

For permission to include material of which they control the copyright grateful acknowledgment is made to the following: Yale University Press for extensive quotations from *The Memorial Quadrangle* by Robert Dudley French, from *Yale, A History* by Brooks M. Kelley, and from *A Connecticut Yankee* by Wilbur L. Cross; *Yale Alumni Magazine* for "From the Editor's Window" by Frederick W. Bronson; Random House for *One Man's Education* by Wilmarth S. Lewis; and for "A Shropshire Lad" by A. E. Housman, reprinted by permission of Henry Holt & Co., LLC, from *The Collected Poems of A. E. Housman*, © 1965 by Henry Holt & Co.

Yale, A Celebration celebrates not only Yale but its three hundredth anniversary in 2001. We are pleased that this book should be a part of a distinguished list of Tercentennial publications.

Contents

Note and Acknowledgments   6

Foreword   9

I.   In the Beginning   13

II.   A Sense of Place   25

III.   Across Yale's Years   41

IV.   In Youth Rejoice   63

V.   A Liberal Education   77

VI.   The Spirit of Yale   89

Index   109

J'AI SEULEMENT FAICT icy un amas de fleurs estrangières, n'y ayant fourny du mien que le filet à les lier.

I HAVE GATHERED a posie of other men's flowers, and naught but the thread that binds them is my own.

MONTAIGNE

Foreword

IN THIS BOOK, we hear the voices of beloved faculty, devoted deans, and many of my predecessors—voices that evoke Yale's aspirations over 300 years. The book does not attempt to create a complete portrait of the University, but Yale's enduring commitments to teaching, community, and the advancement of knowledge are discernible. The fun and the seriousness of the place also come through clearly.

This compilation by J. Kenneth Brody, Yale College Class of 1944 and Yale Law School Class of 1949, and his daughter Alison, Yale College Class of 1995, was conceived as their gift for the University's Tercentennial. Having seen a similar volume during Alison's postgraduate year at Oxford University, they concluded that Yale deserved no less. Although their effort on Yale's behalf is exceptional, it is also emblematic of the work of thousands of alumni who give time and effort to Yale every year. I am pleased that the Brodys selected Leslie Ansteth Colonna, an artist who spent much of her career in New Haven; this reflects the University's intensified collaboration with those in New Haven and the region.

As Yale moves into its fourth century, this book gives us cause to celebrate and lessons to remember.

RICHARD C. LEVIN, President

Phelps Gateway

ACROSS THE QUIET REACHES of the Common he went slowly, incredibly, toward these strange shapes in brick and stone. The evening mist had settled. They were things undefined and mysterious, things as real as the things of his dreams. He passed through the portals of Phelps Hall, hearing above his head for the first time the echoes of his own footsteps against the resounding vault.

Behind him remained the city, suddenly hushed. He was on the campus, the Brick Row at his left; in the distance the crowded line of the fence, the fence where he later should sit in joyful conclave. Somewhere there in the great protecting embrace of these walls were the friends that should be his, that should pass with him through those wonderful years of happiness and good fellowship that were coming.

"And this is it—this is Yale," he said reverently, with a little tightening of his breath.

They had begun at last—the happy, care-free years that everyone proclaimed. Four glorious years, good times, good fellows, and a free and open fight to be among the leaders and leave a name on the roll of fame. Only four years, and then the world with its perplexities and grinding trials.

"Four years," he said softly. "The best, the happiest I'll ever know! Nothing will ever be like them—nothing!"

OWEN JOHNSON, 1912

It SHOULD NOT BE the function of Yale
to reflect American life, but to lead it.

WILLIAM CLYDE DeVane

In the Beginning

Divinity School

SEE, in each village, treasur'd volumes stand!
And spread pure knowledge through th' enlighten'd land;
Knowledge, the wise Republic's standing force,
Subjecting all things, with resistless course;
That bids the ruler hold a righteous sway,
And bends persuaded freemen to obey.
Frequent, behold the rich Museum yield
The wonders dread of Nature's fruitful field!
See strong invention engines strange devise,
And ope the mysteries of earth, seas, and skies;
Aid curious art to finish works refin'd,
And teach abstrusest science to mankind.

from "Greenfield Hill"
TIMOTHY DWIGHT, 1769

Chapel Street

THREE HUNDRED YEARS since the . . . settlers snatched their first, perilous sustenance from these fields and woods; and in that time, under frost and heat, under blue skies and gray, the land has blossomed and prospered. It has yielded good grain for the millstones of Killingsworth and Saybrook and Branford; it has given up its wood and stone for buildings of every conceivable sort; it has grown villages and towns and cities; and it has produced men.

Not the least surprising growth that has appeared along this stretch of sea-coast is the city of New Haven and what it contains. The little settlement must have looked unpromising enough after its first winter of existence. It was in 1637 that Theophilus Eaton, acting as scout for John Davenport, explored the harbor at the mouth of the Quinnipiac and raised a few shacks on the mud flats along the river bank; but when Davenport himself arrived in the following March, to consolidate his new empire, there were discouraging tales to meet his pioneer's enthusiasm. Winters in this new haven were severe and treacherous, he learned,—as all the sons of Yale have learned, to their sorrow, in their turn. Bleak fogs and unwholesome drizzles bred agues and set the bones aching and the body shuddering. . . .

Still, the harbor was a good one, and the land curved back from it in a broad crescent, rising gently toward two red hills, which stood some three miles inland. There must be rich soil in this broad sweep of plain. Here, if anywhere, New England might be made to blossom and take on the vesture of a promised land. And doubtless, for this special occasion, the versatile climate of Connecticut produced one of those rare days of gold and blue, which descend sometimes like a spell upon New Haven, enchanting the whole landscape into dancing radiance.

By such arts the excellent Mr. Davenport was bewitched and this curving strip of land, lying in the arm of the red hills, was the place he selected for his settlement in the new world.

ROBERT DUDLEY FRENCH, 1929

Davenport College

AMONG THE DREAMS that John Davenport had brought with him out of England—especially out of Coventry, where he had been a pupil at the free school, or out of Oxford, where he took his degree—was the dream of a community that gave all its sons the benefits of learning; and quite early in the history of the new colony, he took pains to provide school and schoolmaster for the young. On the central square of the settlement, probably just northeast of the present site of the United Church, Dominie Cheever opened his schoolhouse in 1644; and New Haven began to grope its way, under the impulse of frequent birchings, toward a position as a place of learning. It was no very liberal curriculum which Cheever's school provided, but it was stern and thoroughgoing and laid steady foundations for a higher educational venture.

ROBERT DUDLEY FRENCH, 1929

IT WAS IN SAMUEL RUSSELL'S parsonage at Branford, probably in October, 1701, that a number of clergymen from the sparse settlements of Connecticut, met and made a gift of books "for the founding of a College in this Colony." The project of a Connecticut college, which had languished as the ghost of a dream since John Davenport had left New Haven in 1668, had recently been galvanized into new life through the energy of this group of clergymen. Their leader, it would appear, was the minister of the church at New Haven, a young James Pierpont, who had married Davenport's granddaughter and had inherited the books which the founder of New Haven had collected for a possible college library. There must have been earlier meetings of this group for the discussion of the project, but the gift of books at Branford, whether it was made in kind or merely by promise, was their first deliberate act toward the realization of their ideal. It has been sufficient, at any rate, to give Branford its place of honor in the annals of Yale, as the birthplace of the college.

ROBERT DUDLEY FRENCH, 1929

WHEREAS several well-disposed and Publick spirited Persons for their sincere Regard to and Zeal for upholding and Propagating of the Christian Protestant Religion by a succession of Learned and Orthodox men have expressed by Petition their earnest desires that full liberty and Privilege be granted to certain Undertakers for the founding, suitably endowing and ordering a Collegiate School within his Majesty's Colony of Connecticut wherein Youth may be instructed in the Arts and Sciences who through the blessing of Almighty God may be fitted for Publick employment both in Church & Civil State.

To the intent thereof that all due encouragement be Given to such Pious Resolutions and that so necessary & Religious an Undertaking may be set forward, supported and well managed. . . .

An Act for Liberty to Erect a Collegiate School,
October 15, 1701

AND SO, with the Church and the Law standing by, the infant Yale was born into stormy New England. Puritanism of a very starchy sort was midwife to this new birth, and the infant was looked to as heir to the stiffest traditions of puritan orthodoxy. Harvard College, which was now approaching adolescence, was manifestly becoming obstreperous and heterodox, to the great distress of Cotton Mather and others among her graduates. It was agreed that this youngster should be carefully guarded against all that, and there was hope that he might yet grow up into a stout champion of the Truth against these Harvard infidels.

ROBERT DUDLEY FRENCH, 1929

WE WHOSE NAMES are hereunto subscribed upon the most serious and deliberate Considerations concerning the present state of the Collegiate School are of the Opinion if it cannot be continued at Saybrook, then it is very convenient if it be settled at New-Haven and therefore do recommend it to all who are generously inclined to promote such settlement of said School that they will please to subscribe what sums they will contribute toward the settlement and support thereof at the Town of New-Haven so reasonably as that it may be offered at ye meeting of ye Trustees next Commencement.

July, 1716

WE ARE COME, now, it will be seen, to the accomplishment of John Davenport's dream and the establishment of the college in his city of New Haven. Obstacles not a few were placed in the way, as the project neared fulfilment, and for a season there was defection among the students themselves, with a rival establishment in full blast at Wethersfield. But forceful hands were shaping the destinies of the college, and a strong personality was at work to compose all differences and to establish a reunited school in the spot that should always have been its home.

ROBERT DUDLEY FRENCH, 1929

HERE IS MR. YALE, formerly Governor of Ft. George in the Indies, who has got a prodigious estate and now by Mr. Dixwell sends forth a relation of his from Connecticut to make him his heir, having no son. He told me lately that he intended to bestow a charity upon some College in Oxford, under certain restrictions which he mentioned. But I think he should much rather do it to your college, seeing he is a New England and I think a Connecticut man—if therefore when his kinsman comes over, you will write him a proper letter on that subject, I will take care to press it home.

JEREMIAH DUMMER
to Rev. James Pierpont
May 22, 1711

THE COLONY OF CONNECTICUT, having for some years a college at Saybrook without a collegious way of living for it, have lately begun to erect a large edifice for it in the town of New Haven. The charge for that expensive building is not yet all paid nor are there any funds of revenues for salaries to the Professors and Instructors to this society. Sir, though you have your felicities in your family, which I pray God continue and multiply, yet certainly, if what is forming at New Haven might wear the name of YALE COLLEGE, it would be better than a name of sons and daughters. And your munificence might easily obtain for you such a commemoration and perpetuation of your valuable name, which would indeed be much better than an Egyptian pyramid.

COTTON MATHER
to Elihu Yale
February 14, 1718

THE AFFAIR of our School hath been in a Condition of Pregnancy: Painfull with a witness have been the Throwes thereof in this General Assembly; But we just now hear, that after the Violent Pangs threatening the Very life of the Babe, Divine Providence as a kind Obstetrix mercifully brought the Babe into the World, & behold A Man-child is born, whereat We all Rejoyce.

JEREMIAH DUMMER
to Elihu Yale, 1717

SO, AFTER MANY DARK DAYS, the Collegiate School had passed at length out of the region of storms, and the June sun smiled upon it. The quarrel over the site was now most happily composed; the need of books had been most satisfactorily supplied; a godfather from overseas had come forward with his gift most opportunely for the christening. Across the street from the market place where John Davenport's first church had stood, the grand new college hall was ready, painted a cerulean blue. In the early summer of 1718, tutors and student body—less than a score, all told—entered into their new home and took upon them collectively the name of Yale, descended upon them from the portly Elihu, Indian merchant and nabob, who now, after all his ventures, lies at rest in Wrexham churchyard, across the seas in Wales.

ROBERT DUDLEY FRENCH, 1929

Saybrook College

Born in America, in Europe bred,
In Africa travell'd and in Asia wed,
Where long he lived, and thriv'd; at London, dead
Much good, some ill, he did; so hope's all even,
And that his soul through mercy's gone to heaven.
You that survive and read, take care
For this most certain exit to prepare:
For only the actions of the just
Smell sweet and blossom in the dust.

Epitaph of Elihu Yale

A LIBRARY is a summons to scholarship.
The library is the heart of the University.

Inscription, Sterling Memorial Library

A Sense of Place

Pierson College

'Neath the Elms

Winds of night around us sighing,
In the elm trees murmur low,
In the elm trees murmur low
Let no ruder sounds replying,
Break our happy voices' flow,
Tra la la la.
'Tis a jolly life we lead
Care and trouble we defy;
Let the short-lived hours speed,
Running smoothly, quickly by;
Til the darkness fades away,
And the morning light we hail,
We will sing with cheerful hearts,
Songs of home, songs of home and of Yale,
Of dear old Yale, tra la la la.

Listen! faintly chiming,
O'er the river's placid breast,
Evening bells are ringing,
Calling us to rest.

See, the full moon, rising, weaves
Robes of light o'er tow'r and hall;
Thro' the slowly lifting leaves
Silver lances flash and fall.
Louder yet the chorus raise,
Friendship lasts when youth must fail,
Jolly, jolly are the days
'Neath the elms, 'Neath the elms of dear old Yale,
'Neath the elms of dear old Yale.

H. Baldwin, 1871

East Rock

ALONG THE CONNECTICUT SHORE of Long Island Sound, the sun falls, here and there, upon islands of rusty granite, where the rocky frame that underlies New England, twisting its surface into narrow valleys or tossing it into mountain heights, breaks through the waters in the midst of the sea. In the sunburnt ledges of these islands, one recognizes something more animated than is usually to be found in the dumb kingdom of the minerals. The weather-beaten granite has an individuality which belongs to this corner of the land and marks it as a stone fit for our builder's purposes. Under every sort of weather—and we have them all in Connecticut—it throws back the light in a warm and friendly glow. Its texture is as rough as homespun, its strength as rugged as the pioneer's; yet in the late afternoon, its surface seems to grow softer and more mellow, under the slanting rays of the sun, much as a face that is usually a little stern and rigid may melt into more genial lines under the influence of friendship. The character of New England is stamped upon this stone.

ROBERT DUDLEY FRENCH, 1929

28

A Proclamation
by His Excellency Wilbur L. Cross, Governor

As the colors of autumn stream down the wind, scarlet in sumach and maple, spun gold in the birches, a splendor of smoldering fire in the oaks along the hill, and the last leaves flutter away, and dusk falls briefly about the worker bringing in from the field a late load of its fruit, and Arcturus is lost to sight and Orion swings upward that great sun upon his shoulder, we are stirred once more to ponder the Infinite Goodness that has set apart for us, in all this moving mystery of creation, a time of living and a home. In such a spirit I appoint Thursday, the twenty-fourth of November a day of

Public Thanksgiving

In such a spirit I call upon the people to acknowledge heartily, in friendly gathering and house of prayer, the increase of the season nearing now its close: the harvest of earth, the yield of patient mind and faithful hand, that have kept us fed and clothed and have made for us a shelter even against the storm. It is right that we whose arc of sky has been darkened by no war hawk, who have been forced by no man to stand and speak when to speak was to choose between death and life, should give thanks also for the further mercies we have enjoyed, beyond desert or an estimation, of Justice, Freedom, Loving-kindness, Peace—resolving, as we prize them, to let no occasion go without some prompting or some effort worthy in a way however humble of those proudest among man's ideals, which burn, though it may be like candles fitfully in our gusty world, with a light so clear we name its source divine.

Wilbur L. Cross
November 12, 1936

THE SCENERY about New Haven—very various, and richly wooded for the neighborhood of so large a town—leaves indelible impressions on all college walkers. Two ridges or dykes of trap end in the fine precipices known as East and West Rock, each about two miles from the university. These with their intermediate spurs look over the plain in which the city lies. They are covered with a growth of red cedar and juniper. Past the foot of each flows a creek bordered by a narrow strip of salt marsh, the hay-stacks on which have been aptly compared by Dr. Holmes to billiard-balls lying about on their tables. The creeks run into a harbor long and narrow, whose entrance is guarded by a point of rocks, jutting out boldly from the groves behind and carrying a lighthouse on its back. When the day is clear, you can see from East Rock the white caps beyond the Light, and across the Sound the line of Long Island sand bluffs. How many a September saunter we remember over the woody Fair Haven hills when the barberries were turning red! How many a draught of the small, small beer at the cheerful toll-gate on the Woodbridge Pike! How many a lazy spring day while on the beach at Morris Cove, under the row of half-dead Lombardy poplars, watching the ripples curling in over the sand! Here the vernal impulse would seize us, prompting Homeric voyages to the Thimbles, and making us impatient for the return of those summer midnights when, in the deadest of calms, we should float up the bay on a flood-tide toward "White's" trying to discover by the phosphorescence in the wake, and by our scarcely receding cigar-smoke as it rose to the stars, whether our rudder was making any progress through the water.

HENRY A. BEERS, 1910

New Haven Green

THE SECRET of our content with Yale's location probably lies in the nickname City of Elms. There's nothing like tall trees along the sidewalks to make a city seem like the Great Outdoors. Especially elms.

New Haveners have always appreciated their city's elms. What's more, they planted a lot of them. The famous Pierpont elms (1686)—a pair of giants that lived more than 150 years and reached a circumference of 18 feet. And the 80-foot Franklin elm planted beside the Town Pump April 17, 1790, the day Ben Franklin died. The first planting of trees on the Green (buttonwood & elms) took place in 1759. In 1792 James Hillhouse (The Old Sachem) laid out his Avenue and planted elms along it, helped on occasion by a youth who later became President Day of Yale. About that time the Old Sachem needled the community into planting more trees on the Green, most of them from the Hillhouse Farm in Meriden. Again in 1837 the townsfolk planted 150 maples and elms on the Green.

Wrote New Haven historian George Dudley Seymour in 1911: "In 1850 the Green presented a wholly different and far more beautiful picture than it does today. The elms on the Green—that great elm-gallery—once so famous and now a thing of the past, did not, as I think, reach their greatest perfection until as late as 1865, but their beauty had been the wonder and admiration of travelers for years prior to 1850."

FREDERICK W. BRONSON, 1968

NEW HAVEN! Smoky, dirty, dull, small: not the beautiful New Hampshire hills where I went to school, not exciting New York City, just gray and dreary urban Connecticut. My roommate and school friend Ben Tilghman and I shared a room in Wright Hall on the ground floor, situated on the Old Campus above the Post Office, which was called Yale Station. The feel of that old part of the campus was Victorian, like my father's bedroom and my grandmother's house. Grand, dark brownstone dormitories surrounded it. Elm trees shaded the grass; the wooden Yale Fence lined flagstone paths. Battell Chapel, superbly hideous, was in one corner. At the other end stood the two remaining Colonial brick buildings. In front of one a statue of Yale alumnus Nathan Hale, clean cut, handsome in his long hair and Colonial dress, took its natural place at the door of the freshman office. The inscription on the pedestal read "I regret I only have one life to give for my country." He was the archetypal Yale man. I felt Nathan Hale probably would have regretted he only had one life to give for Yale.

This was manhood. Coming here was a rite of passage. My father always referred to Princeton *boys* and Yale *men*. Princeton boys never grew up, he said (partly true!). Harvard men, he said, spent too much time with social clubs and debutante parties worrying about whose family was really good and whose family was just rich. Harvard men drank too much.

But Yale was different, he pointed out: a male society working hard all week at studies and outside activities for the college. You were expected to go out for athletics, or singing, or debating or Dwight Hall, the organization sponsoring good works. You were to "pull your weight" as a Yale citizen. This would equip you for later life, and without it you could not be tapped for a senior society, a dreadful thought meant to strike fear in our hearts.

Given my father's mastery of all this mythic material, I was not surprised that the new president of Yale, Charlie Seymour, was his classmate. I was not in the least surprised that Dad knew God.

PAUL MOORE, 1982

YET THE LIFE of Yale knows some seclusion, as the academic life always must. Though the streets surround us, and commerce barks at our gates, we have not forgone all intimacy and retirement. As the city has grown in upon us, we have built with more foresight than at first appears, creating seclusion for ourselves by erecting our buildings at the boundaries of our grounds and leaving open space within. For colleges situated like ours, in the heart of a city, the quadrangle yields seclusion without attempting isolation. The Old Brick Row of the nineteenth century lay too open to the city, as Timothy Dwight had the wisdom to perceive; and college life, having its center at the fence along the corner of College and Chapel Streets, was thrown into a publicity which threatened to descend into something all too like the corner loafer's existence. Connecticut Hall, the only survivor of the Row, stands today in dignified seclusion within the college close. The gates of our Campus are but rarely shut, yet we pass through them into intimacy such as no quiet hilltop could better afford us. The Quadrangle has been a characteristic feature of Yale building for many years, and the Memorial Buildings carry on a tradition that has grown old at Yale and has had far greater antiquity in other college communities.

ROBERT DUDLEY FRENCH, 1929

Timothy Dwight College

WALK THROUGH YALE. Learn her lessons. On every carefully constructed facade, knowledge faces you with marbled eyes. Read the writing on the walls around you. In the words of Branford, facing Jonathan Edwards, "The truth shall set me free."

Beinecke Plaza

I cross the street to Woolsey. Within, thousands of names speak a still language: "This was a life." Under the doorway I read, "Peace crowns their act of sacrifice." The Rotunda shares a shy hope—there is no room left for the names of the dead from another war.

Beinecke Plaza is silent, with the hush of a crowded cathedral, or a late-night city snow. Its language lacks words. The rich chatter of freshmen within disturbs the Grecian sanctity of this building, the most grand, most serene on campus. Argonne, Chateau-Thierry, Ypres. Names add ages to Commons, making it seem ancient. It will endure.

On the lawn of Cross Campus I feel architecture's subliminal seduction. The pointing turrets of Sterling Library, the countless pinnacles of the Law School, the loftiness of Harkness conspire against me. In subtle undertones, the spirit of the university rains down in whispers—"Spire!" Inspiration, Aspiration. Perspiration.

In the library, self-proclaimed "heart of the university," vaulted arches jump to distant heights. The windows' mullions arc upwards like pillars. Ceilings soar three stories above us, leaving room for perpetual growth.

The writing on the walls and the lessons of the buildings are etched in stone. Listen to the silence.

TINA KELLY, 1983

34

Hillhouse Avenue

THE DAYS ARE GONE that I dreamed away beneath the green arcades of the fair Elm City. But still come the budding spring and the blooming summer to embower those quiet old streets and fill the morning hour with birds' sweet singing. Still comes the gorgeous autumn—the dead summer laid in state—and the cloud-robed winter to round the circling year. Still streams the golden sunlight through the green canopies of tented elms, and still, I ween, do pretty school-girls loiter there along in flirting fascination, through the dreamy holiday afternoons, beneath their shade. Still do our memories haunt those old walks we loved so well; the avenue, shaded and silent, like a grove of Academe, fit dwelling of colloquial man of science and genial metaphysician; the old Cemetery with its brown ivy-mantled wall, its dark massive evergreens, and moss-grown grave-stones, that before years had effaced their inscriptions, told the brief story of early settlers; elm-arched Temple-street, where the mid-night moon shone so softly through the dark masses of foliage, and slept so sweetly on the sloping green. Still do those old wharves and ware-houses, ancient haunts of colonial commerce and scenes of continental struggle, rest there in their quietude, hearing but murmurs of the noisy merchant-world without; and the fair bay lies silent among those green hills that slope southward to the Sound.

The Knickerbocker, 1856

35

Harkness Quadrangle

THE WORKMAN from a foreign land,
Who chiseled out this cusp and foil,
Has, with unconsciousness of toil,
Prisoned himself to this fair soil,
With bonds more strong than laws command.

And when this stone has fallen low,
Eroded by the passing years,
There will be those among the seers,
Who, looking back upon their peers,
Will marvel that such things were so.

WILLIAM DOUGLAS, 1918

Sheffield Sterling Strathcona Hall

IT IS HARKNESS TOWER that first catches the eye of the visitor to the Quadrangle. Perhaps he has had a glimpse of its crown as he has entered New Haven, and the unusual nature of that apparition, rising above the housetops of the modern city, has drawn him through the streets toward the college. At the corner of Church and Chapel Streets, the profile of the tower becomes clearly visible, behind the spires of the churches on Temple Street and the turrets of Phelps Hall; and the city suddenly takes on dignity, as a place of venerable traditions. About the Green, the burnished pigeons circle and fall, in waves of flashing color and the air is full of the whirring of their wings and the gentle murmur of their peace. They settle about the crosswalks that lead the traveler across the Green, and hardly stir out of his path as he saunters among them—past Center Church, past the grave where the Regicide lies buried—till he comes into the shade of the elms beyond Temple Street and approaches the buildings of the college. Then he passes through the archway to Phelps Hall, and Harkness Tower stands before him, only half veiled by the elms of the Campus. He has not seen its like anywhere upon this continent. Centuries of time and a complete revolution in men's ways of living and of thinking separate him from the distant age, when such towers as this first grew out of the daring of man's imagination; but across the interval of years, the beauty that the Gothic builders made, out of the darkness and the light that were in them, stretches out its strong, graceful hands and catches at his heart.

ROBERT DUDLEY FRENCH, 1929

Jonathan Edwards College

LIBRARY STREET encourages the visitor to savor the smaller, more intimate features of Neo-Gothic architecture. Two small bridges cross the ivy-filled moat of Branford College to the walkway. The gate honors John Davenport, the founder of the New Haven Colony, and his follower, James Pierpont, the principal founder of Yale. The inviting low bay windows of Branford and the dormer windows of Jonathan Edwards light the walkway at night. The only major decorative feature is a small relief sculpture of St. George with his lance poised to attack the dragon. In all, the scene was created to invoke the early days of Oxford, a time of beginnings and a respite from the world of the city.

JUDITH ANN SCHIFF, 1991

WELL, this is what the town has been coming to: that it should take its place among the cities that men seek out instinctively, as reminder and assurance of the better things of life. As you wind your way up the valley of the Thames, the tower of Magdalen lifts it head above the tree tops, proudly confident of the high things it shadows forth. Across the fens of Cambridgeshire, as you come down the road from Ely, a cluster of towers breaks the even sky line, not so rich, perhaps, with the last enchantments of the Middle Ages as the towers of Oxford, but just as comforting to men and women who have been going to and fro on the earth, and walking up and down in it, and have found few cities where light and truth have been cherished as in this Cambridge, through the discords of the warring centuries. Shall we be too modest (or too hypocritical), while the Harkness Tower stands before us, to admit our hope that henceforward New Haven may have some right to take its place in the company of Oxford and Cambridge? We know what Yale has been saying to her sons, through the last two centuries; we believe that they are things which all men delight to hear; and now, after years of waiting, they are at last visible to the world, in storm-enduring stone.

ROBERT DUDLEY FRENCH, 1929

AND THERE SHALL LINGER other magic things,—
The fog that creeps in wanly from the sea,
The rotten harbor smell, the mystery
Of moonlight elms, the flash of pigeon wings,
The sunny Green, the old-world peace that clings
About the college yard where endlessly
The dead go up and down. These things shall be
Enchantment of our heart's rememberings.

Class Poem, 1915
ARCHIBALD MACLEISH

THY LIGHT and truth shall set me free.

Inscription, Branford College

Across Yale's Years

Harkness Tower

Consule Planco

IN PLANCUS' DAYS, when life was slow,
We dwelt within the Old Brick Row
Before Durfee or Welch was built,
Or gilded youths in Vanderbilt
Looked down upon the mob below.
Then freshmen did not use to go
Most every evening to the show;
Quite inexpensive was our gilt
In Plancus' days.
We had no football then, you know;
All bloodless lay the untrodden snow,
No gore was shed, no ink was spilt,
No poet got upon his stilt
To write these Frenchified rondeaux
In Plancus' days.

HENRY A. BEERS, 1869

THEY HAVE SEEN WAR close at hand, too, when the Redcoats, under General Tryon and "traitor Arnold," marched upon New Haven in 1779. On that occasion, in devotion to their foster-city, the students at the college demanded arms of the Selectmen, that they might go out with Captain Hillhouse and the Guards to dispute the crossing of West River with the invader; but only a few of them were able to secure weapons. Among the stoutest-hearted of New Haven's defenders, however, was the venerable Naphtali Daggett, former President of the college, who took down his fowling piece from the chimney, mounted his old black mare, and rode forth to engage the enemy.

Connecticut Hall

A British officer, startled and amused at the apparition of this Nestor in the opposing host, cried out to him, in the midst of the affray, "What are you doing here, you old fool, firing on His Majesty's troops?" "Exercising the rights of war," replied the Livingston Professor of Divinity.

"If I let you go this time, you old rascal," said the Britisher, "will you ever fire again on the troops of His Majesty?"

"Nothing more likely," was Dr. Daggett's reply. Indeed, the earnest old patriot had to be dislodged from his station by force and was driven into town at the point of the bayonet.

ROBERT DUDLEY FRENCH, 1929

AGREED That every Barrel of Beer delivered to the Butler @ 8/pr Barrel shall be made of Half a Bushel of good Barley Malt after it is ground or a Bushel of good Oat Malt after it is ground or a peck of good Barley Malt after it is ground and a Quart of good Molasses or half a Bushel of good Oat Malt after it is ground & a quart of good Molasses & be mash't and well brewed & hopped.

AGREED That the Steward of this College shall for the Year ensuing pay to the Butler of the same fourty shillings pr Quarter as a Reward for his Service in dealing out the Commons of Bread and Beer to the Scholars.

AGREED That the Butler of the College shall for the Year ensuing pay to the Treasurer of the College fourty Shillings pr Quarter on the Account of ye Lost Commons of Bread & Beer which are by this Act allowed to said Butler.

Proceedings of the Trustees
September 12, 1783

6. IF ANY SCHOLAR shall play at Dice or Cards, or even any lawful Play, or Wager, or shall call any strong Drink in a Tavern within two Miles of College, except in Company with his Father or Guardian, he shall be punished, for the first Offence, two Shillings and six Pence; for the second five Shillings; and for the third may be expelled. And if a Scholar without Leave from the President or his Tutor, shall bring into College, or into his Chamber in Town, any Rum, Wine, or any other strong Drink, he may be fined, not exceeding the Value of the Drink brought in, or otherwise punished as he shall deserve.

7. If any Scholar shall damnify the College House, Glass, Fence, or any Thing belonging to the College, he shall be fined a Shilling, and make good the Damages; and if the Crime be repeated, shall pay double Damages.

8. Every Scholar in studying Time is required wholly to abstain from Singing, loud Talking and Noisiness, upon Penalty of our Peace, And if any other Scholar shall at any Time make an indecent Rout, Tumult, Noise, or Hallowing, or call out aloud, to any other Scholar, in the Presence of the President or a Tutor, he shall be punished not exceeding two Shillings.

9. If any Scholar shall play at Hand-Ball, or Foot-Ball, or Bowls in the College Yard, or throw any Thing against College, by which the Glass may be endangered or shall pour Water in any College Entry, he shall be punished six Pence, and make good the Damages.

10. If any Scholar shall anywhere act a Comedy or a Tragedy, he shall be fined three Shillings, one Shilling if he shall be present at the acting of one; and if in acting he shall put on Women's Apparel, he shall be publickly admonished.

Chapter IV, Laws of Yale College, 1774

THEY STROLLED OVER to the fence where, along Chapel and College streets, were little groups of students, some talking, some singing, and almost everyone smoking pipes or cigarettes.

"This is the famous fence," said Uncle Dick. "It is very convenient to sit on. You can just catch your heels on the second round very nicely. It's as comfortable as an easy-chair. This is where the social life of the college centers. I hope it will never be removed, though the disposition on the part of the faculty is to remove it and disperse these daily gatherings. In my opinion the splendid democracy of old Yale will receive a blow the moment the fence is gone. Here a man shows what's in him, forms his lasting friendships, and shows what he really is to his classmates."

Harry and his friends perched on the fence, and the former felt a secret thrill of joy as his Uncle Lyman went on:

"We are now sitting on the senior fence. Below that gateway there is the junior, as far as the corner. Then around the corner comes the sophomore fence. Freshmen have no fence."

"Why not?" asked Harry, apparently much grieved. "There's lots of room for them?"

"Well—you see, it would be dangerous. You are too young to roost on it. You'd only fall off and hurt yourselves," laughed his uncle. "Toward the end of the year the sophs move over to the junior fence and the freshmen have a chance at it, but it is always a matter of favor to them and depends, I believe, on whether they beat Harvard at baseball."

JOHN SEYMOUR WOOD, 1894

*Stiles and
Morse Colleges*

Brave Mother Yale

FAIRER than love of woman,
Stronger than pride of gold,
Stands, nor shall fail, love for old Yale,
Mother of love untold
Mother of love, proudly we call thee,
Singing together adown the long line,
Light from above ever befall thee!
Hear thou and cheer thou the hearts that are thine.

Beacon of truth uplifted
Set in the northern sea,
While yet they live, thy sons shall give
Honor and love to thee,
Star of our hope, shine on forever!
Naught can the calm of thy radiance pale.
Guarding thee yet, failing thee never
Still shall we love our brave mother, Old Yale.

CHARLES EDMUND MERRILL
THOMAS G. SHEPARD, 1903

PRESENTATION DAY was a senior festival which marked the closing of their active college life. Before 1869 it had been held for nearly one hundred and fifty years. After the final examinations were completed a college official presented to the President for their degrees those candidates who had been successful. The speech was given in Latin with the President responding in the same language. In the earlier days punch was drunk by the officers and students to celebrate the event. Several hours afterwards the assembly of ladies and gentlemen met in the chapel. The President opened the exercises with another Latin speech and the names of the seniors were read, but this was given up after 1861. There followed speeches by students. All this took about an hour.

At half past one all assembled in Alumni Hall for a cold luncheon.

In the afternoon the seniors lounged on the grass or brought out benches and there they smoked the pipe of peace, sang songs written for the occasion, joking, laughing and disporting themselves as best they might. After planting the class ivy on one of the buildings they attended evening chapel. Later they went to the campus, formed a ring, smoked their pipes which were then broken, and said good-bye to each other.

LOOMIS HAVEMEYER, 1960

Blue Roses of Academus

So late and long the shadows lie
    Under the quadrangle wall:
From such a narrow strip of sky
    So scant an hour the sunbeams fall,
    They hardly come to touch at all
    This cool, sequestered corner where,
    Beside the chapel belfry tall,
I cultivate my small parterre.

Poor, sickly blooms of Academe,
    Recluses of the college close,
Whose nun-like pallor would beseem
The violet better than the rose:
    There's not a bud among you blows
With scent or hue to lure the bee:
    Only the thorn that on you grows—
Only the thorn grows hardily.

Pale cloisterers, have you lost so soon
    The way to blush. Do you forget
How once, beneath the enamored moon,
    You climbed against the parapet,
    To touch the breast of Juliet
Warm with a kiss, wet with a tear,
    In gardens of the Capulet,
Far south, my flowers, not here—not here?

Henry A. Beers, 1910

IN THE COLLEGE YEAR 1883–84, Yale gained a triple victory, winning the intercollegiate championships in football and baseball, and the boat race with Harvard on the Thames. . . . Victories on the gridiron and the diamond were easily won. . . . But as the time was approaching for the boat race, few if any of us expected that the crew could win. . . . But Harry Flanders, of our class, who was elected captain for the next year, carefully trained his crew, without talking about it, to a longer and lower stroke and won over Harvard by 4 lengths. He had achieved the impossible and was a hero to every one of us.

The news of that memorable day (June 27, 1884) came over the wire just before six o'clock. Within a few minutes the chimes of Battell Chapel were set a ringing and the Campus by the fence was quickly crowded with students shouting and jumping with joy. Soon horns were blowing and cannon crackers were bursting at our feet and over our heads; while a wild procession of students began a march around the Campus to the noisy music of drums. By that time the excitement was spreading through the city. The chimes of Trinity Church struck up "Here's to Good Old Yale" and the bells of Center Church and the First Methodist Church rang out the victory. Before darkness came on, merchants along Chapel Street decorated their stores with bunting and the Stars and Stripes were flung to the breeze.

An immense throng of students met the returning crew at the railway station and, led by a brass band, escorted them, as they sat dressed in white flannel suits in open carriages, all the way to the college fence, burning Roman candles and red lights in front of them as if they were demigods. When they reached the fence the Campus was ablaze with a huge bonfire of tar barrels, and a cannon installed on the Green was firing a salute while hoarse voices were sending up cheer after cheer in a continuous volley. On a signal the noise subsided and a leader, stepping into the street, proposed three times three for Captain Flanders and after that a long cheer for each member of the victorious crew. Then under the glare of red lights the crew were taken over to the New Haven House for supper and a brief rest, to return an hour or two later to the Campus for a celebration which lasted until the break of morning.

As I took my last look at the Campus flooded with light from the bonfire, rising and falling through giant elms and over the face of the long brick row, I felt an exhilaration which transcended the glare and noise of a celebration over an athletic victory. Did my imagination vaguely transmute the real scene into a vision of historic Yale where generations of young men have come in their search for the light of truth, and afterwards departed with gifts that Yale bestowed upon them? *Lux et Veritas.* I do not know. All I know is:

Bliss was it in that dawn to be alive
But to be young was very Heaven!

WILBUR L. CROSS, 1943

OF ONE THING they were sure, that there was hardly a spot in New Haven quite so attractive as the corner of Chapel and College Streets

That corner had a border of low fence with two round rails. Those round rails had some paint on them, but most of that which had once and again at long intervals been given them was scattered in infinitesimal proportions among the trousers of Yale men. Back of that fence was a stretch of bare ground, trod by the sons of Eli from time immemorial. Over all were the arching elms, which had withstood the bonfires of victories from a least as far back as the first race won against Harvard, when Mr. Twichell himself pulled an oar; which had shaded innumerable concourses both formal and impromptu; which had sifted the harmonies and moonbeamed the sentiments of a thousand summer evenings; which had guarded the home-comings of the sons of Yale from the time they first sat in fifties or hundreds, with trembling and great joy, on the newly won rails, till they gathered feeble and few, at fourscore, for their last reunion.

WALTER CAMP, 1899

MANY YEARS have passed since those days in 1863 when a few venturesome youths, on their way to and from the Boat House in the harbor discovered, by accident, the Moriarty's hospitable ale house on Wooster Street. From this accidental discovery came the "Mory's" of today operated as a club in the interests of its undergraduate and alumni members who meet in common fellowship to perpetuate the traditions of the old and new Yale.

What college or university possesses an undergraduate and alumni club comparable in character to "Mory's" with its distinctive environment and traditions? Once inside its swinging "Temple Bar" doors your attention is directed to printed and pictorial reminders of the undergraduate social and athletic activities of the new and old Yale, to the table tops with their carvings of "Whiffenpoofs" and of Yale men of this and other generations, to the fireplace and mantel on and over which repose the old clock, *Banners* and *Pot Pourris*, and other reminders of "The Quiet House" and "Temple Bar" days.

GEORGE E. THOMPSON, 1938

FRESHMAN RESTRICTIONS

THE FRESHMAN is not allowed by college custom to (a) to smoke a pipe in the street or campus, (b) to carry a cane before Washington's birthday, (c) to dance at the Junior Promenade, (d) to sit on the college Fence, (e) to play ball or spin tops on the campus.

WALTER CAMP, 1899

THE DEED of Joseph E. Sheffield, Esq., dated October, 1858, conveying to this Corporation the stone building on the northeast corner of Grove and Prospect streets in this city, with a piece of land thereto attached, for the uses and purposes of the Scientific School at the College, be accepted on the conditions stated in said deed; and it was ordered that the grateful acknowledgments of the Corporation be presented to Mr. Sheffield for this magnificent gift.

Vote of the Corporation
July 26, 1859

Calhoun College

JUNIOR PROMENADE.—The most important social event of the year is the Junior Promenade, which occurs in the second term, just previous to Lent. It is gotten up in the most elegant manner, by a committee of the leading society men of the junior class appointed especially for that purpose. Neither pains nor expense are spared. Even the minutest details receive the utmost care. Elegant cards of invitation are issued, on which appears the class numeral disposed with great taste, while the order of dances, etc., displays the highest skill of the "art preservative." Carll's Opera House is the scene of the festivities, which are attended by fashion and beauty from all sections of the country. No event of the kind, anywhere, excels the magnificence of the Junior Promenade at Yale, and no college event, except Commencement, attracts so large an attendance of visitors. The influx is very noticeable about the College for two or three days previous to the Promenade, and the most casual observer cannot but notice the air of festivity which prevails. Many of those who have come for the purpose of being present at the Promenade attend college prayers, during their stay, at Battell Chapel, occupying the spacious galleries.

W.E. DeCrow, 1884

ON APRIL FIRST, all Yale welcomed Mr. William Howard Taft at the railroad station with a terrific Yale cheer, marched behind his automobile in a triumphal procession through the streets of the city and then assembled in the square at Woolsey Hall, to listen to the words of thanks which Mr. Taft—"Mr." for the first time in thirty-five years—pronounced from the balcony of the hall. It was like a reception to a monarch, in a way, for Yale took charge of the entire celebration, cheered their professor-to-be, and in the square cheered themselves hoarse to show some of the appreciation in which Mr. Taft is held.

And a word must be said for Mrs. Taft, the only lady in the entire procession, who, not at all overcome by the attention she was attracting, got out of the automobile at the entrance to the Porter gateway, wearing the large bunch of violets which Captain Spalding of the varsity eleven had presented to her at the train, and at the right hand of her husband strode valiantly through "Grub Street," between the cheering double lines of undergraduates and appeared with Mr. Taft in the balcony, where she sat and watched the proceedings go to their exuberant close.

That Mr. Taft was overcome by the tremendous fervor and sincerity of the reception—in some degree at least—seemed to be shown from the fact that during the procession the familiar smile was not as much in evidence as on former visits here during his occupancy of the presidential office. But when he stepped out on the balcony, looked down on a sea of waving hats, heard the great roaring cheers which rose to him, the smile came back.

Could anyone have put more power into his cheer at that moment he would have done so, for it was a moment historic in its importance to Yale. From that moment it was "Professor" Taft, everyone realized it, and the waves of cheering rose and subsided, rattling back from the perfect sounding board formed by the diverging walls on either side of the balcony.

The Eli Book
1913–14

Woolsey Hall

The New Yale

ALL DAY we hear the chisels ring,
The windlass creak, the masons sing;
With every brightening moon there falls
A longer shadow from the walls.
We hope these rising halls may bring
Some new event—some wished-for thing.
We look to see that not alone
Of mellow brick-work or of stone,
But reared by wisdom's magic wands,
Invisible, not made with hands,
Yet stronger than the trowel builds,
Deep laid by toiling scholar-guilds,
Her corner-stone's free-masonry
As broad as this brave century,
Our new, regenerate Yale shall be—
Our Yankee university.

HENRY A. BEERS, 1871

55

Law School

OUR OWN UNDERGRADU-
ATE ERA witnessed the Hadley-
Angell interchange. (Another pair
of well-groomed Yale Presidents,
by the way). We were long after
Dink Stover's peg-topped pants
and turtleneck sweater but earlier
than Lucius Beebe's frock coat
and topper.

Mustered out of World War I
uniforms, as Freshmen every man-
Jack of us quickly asserted his individuality by donning a little brown hat pulled
down over his ears. By the time we graduated the hats were pearl grey fedo-
ras—a change that seemed instantaneous, like sandpipers flashing silver as they
veer in flight.

Our generation introduced the coonskin coat and unlatched galoshes that
gave the age its trademark. We also featured the Brooks Brothers four-button
suit with belt, waistcoat, knickers, and long pants. Our shirts were Brooks Brothers pullover button-downs, imitated sporadically ever since but never surpassed.
Our favorite shoes were Frank Brothers perforated Cordovans. When it rained
we looked like Uneeda Biscuit ads in yellow slickers that stuck to anything they
touched. Only the Y-Men were privileged to wear those round white hats with
the modest blue letter. And until Tap Day in Junior Year, of course, any one of
us would rather have been caught naked on the Taft Corner than anywhere on
the Campus with his head uncovered.

Harry Rosenberg (later Toasty Rosie) pressed all the clothes we could wear
on a term contract. Our pants were therefore always razor edged. (We also
smelled continually of dry cleaning). Rosey's energetic services wore our clothes
out a little faster so that his friends and relations on Chapel Street could supply
us with more. And more. And more. It cost us money but we dazzled.

FREDERICK W. BRONSON, 1968

THE YALE PRESIDENT must be a Yale man. He must be a person of character with religious convictions. He must be a scholar of international reputation with deep respect for science if he is a humanist and who loves the arts if he is a scientist. He must be a man of the present with knowledge of the past and a clear vision of the future. He must not be too far to the right, too far to the left, or a middle-of-the-roader. Poised, clear-eyed, informed, he must be ready to give the ultimate word on every subject under the sun from how to handle the Russians to why undergraduates riot in the spring. As a speaker he must be profound with a wit that bubbles up and brims over in a cascade of brilliance; his writing must be lucid and cogent, his style both Augustan and contemporary. He must be young enough to have "dynamic ideas," but old enough to be sensible about them; courageous, but not foolhardy. He must be "a great personality," by which is meant one who commands respect, who soothes the ruffled and charms the sentimental, an Olympian who is one of the boys without affectation or jocularity. He must have intimate knowledge of all the University's colleges, schools, departments, institutes, libraries, museums, and special projects, and know how to administer them efficiently and economically, delegating authority while keeping his finger on every pulse and in every pie. He must be a man with a heart who will share the private joys and sorrows of his faculty. Above all, he must be a leader, leading of course in the right direction, which is to money. Morning, noon, and night he must get money; money for salaries, money for buildings, money for scholarships, money for new projects that will prove he is dynamic. Since his job takes eighteen hours a day seven days a week eleven months a year, his health must be good—no colds, no ulcers, no slipped discs. Finally, his wife must be a combination of Queen Victoria, Florence Nightingale, and the Best-Dressed Woman of the Year. As I have been talking you have guessed who the leading candidate is, but there is a question about Him: *Is* God a Yale Man?

WILMARTH S. LEWIS, 1968

Berkeley College

DIFFERENT FROM EACH OTHER we already are, and probably to a greater extent than has been the case with any of the 268 classes that came before you. Not only because, for the first time in the history of Yale both sexes are represented, but also because in recent years, Yale has made ever increasing efforts in order to draw its students from all parts of our society. The result is that every one of you, without exception, is a member of at least one significant minority. Hence the unprecedentedly large and valuable educational benefits which you can derive from living with your fellow students. Hence also the sobering fact that not one of you alone can claim to be truly representative of your class. Indeed, this class will become itself only through the process of transcending diversity by living and working together.

GEORGES MAY, 1969

Ivy Ode

WE ARE GONE from sight
    and mind,
Leaving no token here
    behind
To speak for us in this loved scene,
    O, Ivy, keep our memory green,
And trace in thy soft, leafy line,
The dear old name of Sixty-nine.

When youth and Yale are far away,
And these young heads are growing
    gray,
We'll think, how on this cold stone wall
Our Ivy climbeth strong and tall;
And then our hearts, like thee, shall
    grow
The greener for the winter snow.

Farewell! Farewell! A leaf from thee
In after years a charm shall be
To start the tear in eyes long dry;
To stir the drowsy memory
With sad, sweet thoughts of Auld
    Lang Syne.
And friends we loved in Sixty-nine.

HENRY A. BEERS, Class Day, 1869

Science Hill and Ingalls Rink

A green Pontiac with Arizona plates slowed up and parked on College Street directly under the Editor's window. It was a September afternoon. A pair of skis and an armchair indicated that the Pontiac's load included one entering freshman. The indication was not misleading—eventually Father, Mother, and Junior emerged into the bright New Haven sunlight. We noticed nothing unusual about them and in fact paid them no attention at all until Father, looking up at us with an eager expression, cupped his hands around his mouth and asked: "Can you tell me where Frank Merriwell lived when he was in college?"

FREDERICK W. BRONSON, 1968

Boola

Boola, Boola, Boola, Boola,
Boola, Boola, Boola, Boola,
When we rough-house
Poor old Harvard,
They will holler "Boola Boo!"—Rah, Rah, Rah (spoken),
Oh! Yale, Eli Yale, oh! Yale, Eli Yale!
Oh! Yale, Eli Yale, Oh! Yale, Eli Yale!

ALLAN M. HIRSCH, 1901

Yale is at once a tradition
A company of scholars
A society of friends.

George W. Pierson

In Youth Rejoice

Payne Whitney Gym

Gaudeamus

GAUDEAMUS igitur
Juvenes dum sumus;
Gaudeamus igitur,
Juvenes dum sumus;
Post jucundam juventutem,
Post Molestam senectutem,
Nos habebit humus,
Nos habebit humus.

Ubi sunt, qui ante nos
In mundo fuere?
Transeas ad superos,
Abeas ad inferos
Quos si vis videre.

Alma Mater floreat,
Quae nos educavit,
Caros et commilitones,
Dissitas in regiones
Sparsos congregavit.

Traditional

Old Campus Corner, Wright & Durfee Halls

Wake, Freshmen, Wake

THE STARS, brightly glancing,
Behold us advancing,
And kindly smile upon us from on high;
Our summons awaiting,
With hearts loudly beating,
The Freshmen trembling on their couches lie.

Wake! Wake! Freshmen, wake!
Wake while our song smites the sky;
For now ere we leave you
We heartily give you
A welcome into Delta Beta Xi.

While some sadly ponder,
Still others will wonder
Why we their doors in silence dead pass by;
But, O fortunati!
O terque beati!
Who hear the mystic call of Beta Xi.

Traditional

"THIS IS OLD YALE at its best," said Uncle Dick. "As someone has said, it would be the most delightful place in the world for a fellow to live were it not for its religious and literary exercises. That is its more serious side—what you are really here for, I suppose. But I believe, on the whole, the social life is the most valuable. The classics and mathematics fade out of your life, but the friends you made remain forever."

"I only hope," said Harry solemnly, "that I'll live through the whole four years, and that I'll never be dropped and compelled to go to Harvard!"

"Well, just be—yourself, my boy, and no such calamity will befall you."

JOHN SEYMOUR WOOD, 1894

When I Was One-and-Twenty

WHEN I was one-and-twenty
 I heard a wise man say,
"Give crowns and pounds and guineas
 But not your heart away;
Give pearls away and rubies
 But keep your fancy free."
But I was one-and-twenty,
 No use to talk to me.

When I was one-and-twenty
 I heard him say again,
"The heart out of the bosom
 Was never given in vain;
'Tis paid with sighs a plenty
 And sold for endless rue."
And I am two-and-twenty,
 And oh, 'tis true, 'tis true.

A. E. HOUSMAN

AND THIS SEEMED the most striking thing about the place—how densely packed time was. It went so fast, and yet so much was done, so much learned and accomplished, so many friendships made, so many good times, so many bad. These extremes seemed impossible. How could there be such highs and lows in the same week, even in the same day? You could leave a dinner with friends in Commons and be back in your room feeling lonely in minutes. You could be happy over a new love but then flung into a panic over all the work you had and think you'd never get it done.

The days always seemed like that freshman year. And we went running off to chase our dreams and ourselves with hearts so full and spirits so high that nothing else seemed to matter.

MARTHA BURTON, 1982

University Commons

"Countdown from bow when ready!" The coxswain's voice cut the dawn mist, waking us back to the shell. Hurriedly, I finished tying my feet into the footstretchers and rolled my seat experimentally back and forth along the slide.

"Bow."

"Two."

"Three."

"Four!" I yelled as the count moved through me and up to number eight, the stroke oar. One by one we positioned ourselves at the top of the slide: legs cocked, arms outstretched, blades flat against the water.

Boathouse at Derby

"All eight to row, ready all . . . row!"

In one motion the eight oars flipped into the river, our backs opened and our legs straightened. Hesitantly, but then with more assurance, the boat surged into the current. We were all cold and stiff so early in the morning, yet with each stroke our bodies loosened, fell together. The boat, first pushing through the river, soon lifted with each catch to skim across the ripples as our movements lost self-consciousness to the easy flowing rhythm.

Past the finish line we paddled, past the Rock and past the Harvard camp at Red Top; the landmarks slipped by unnoticed to the beat of the oars. After each stroke, eight new whirlpools traced our path. I thought of nothing, wished for nothing but to put just a little more distance between one set of whirlpools and the next—to make the next stroke a little closer to perfection.

A patch of mist suffused the morning light. Then from nowhere came the rain: hard, driving, a counterpoint to the rhythmic splash of the oars. Their gray carbon fiber matched the water, matched the air. Eric's bare back moved in front of me, the triangle of his deltoids and lats coursing the rain. Surging water, flowing oars and a bare back moving rhythmically before me.

For those moments I could forget where I was, forget the coming race and immerse myself in the pure joy of motion.

Stephen Kiesling, 1982

Good Night, Poor Harvard

GOOD NIGHT, poor Harvard,
Harvard, good night.
We've got your number,
You're high as a kite,
Oh—
Good night, poor Harvard
You're tucked in tight
When the big blue team gets after you
Harvard, good night!

DOUGLAS S. MOORE, 1913

Yale Bowl

Trumbull College

Whoop It Up

FIGHT, fight for Yale,
The sons of Eli are out for glory;
On to the fray,
We'll tell to Harvard the same old story,
The cry is on, on they come
We'll raise the slogan of Yale triumphant
Smash, bang, we'll rip poor Harvard
Whoop it up for Yale today.
The cry is on, on they come,
We'll raise the slogan of Yale triumphant
Smash, bang, we'll rip poor Harvard
Whoop it up for Yale today.

H. G. DODGE
STANLEIGH P. FRIEDMAN, 1906

Student Room Interior

ROOMMATES, it seemed, not only were the basis of most friendships, but also played the most important role of college. . . .

First of all, they provided the gateway to most of the friendships and some of the love affairs in college. Meeting people—the root of education—is much easier when you're introduced in the safety of a foursome. . . .

Roommates were also the companions in the first home-away-from-home for most of us. Eating, sleeping and studying with them made them seem more family than fellow rentiers, and relations seemed to resemble sibling love and rivalry. . . .

But what made roommates so special, and so important, was their being more than just friends, becoming part of Yale itself. This was possible only because of the honesty of room relations. There is something humbling about being seen at eight in the morning, at meals, late at night, drunk, happy, desperate, and relaxed, without the benefit of embellishments. We learned not only who we were but who we were slowly becoming. Tony and I were the only ones who knew what Steve felt when *she* left him, not because he wanted us to know, but because we were there as it happened. Being there was often the most important element of the honesty a room built together.

KEITH HANSEN, 1982

Bingo

Bingo, Bingo
Bingo, Bingo, Bingo, that's the lingo
Eli is bound to win
There's to be a victory, so watch the team begin
B'B'B' Bingo, Bingo,
Harvard's team cannot prevail
Fight! Fight!
Fight with all your might for Bingo Bingo, Eli Yale!

Cole Porter, 1913

The [Yale Political] Union can be of undoubted value to the nation and to the University, provided it maintains independence and voices the true thoughts of those participating. . . Honest debate will help in the search for truthful answers.

Franklin D. Roosevelt

HARKNESS TOWER, bright with moonlight, loomed above me against the clear night sky as I crossed High Street. I could read in the moonlight the words "For God, for Country and for Yale" carved in stone above the Memorial Gate. My footsteps echoed in silence under the archway. The tower threw a long wide shadow across Branford Courtyard. I looked up at the lighted casement windows where the upperclassmen lived. The lights in one room went out and the window was rolled open. Afraid that someone would see me, I moved into the deep shadows closer to the wall. I picked four ivy leaves, careful not to tear the vine. With the leaves in my hands, I trotted out of Branford Courtyard and up High Street.

I started to cross Elm Street in front of Berkeley Oval but I stopped in the middle of the road. The street was quiet without a car or a student around. I began to hum the first few bars of "Night and Day" then, holding high the four ivy leaves I whirled full circle, dancing from the road to the curb to the sidewalk. I knew, no doubt, what it felt like to be Fred Astaire.

MILTON WHITE, 1966

YET AH, that Spring should vanish with the Rose!
That Youth's sweet-scented manuscript should close!
The Nightingale that in the branches sings
Ah whence, and whither flown again, who knows!

OMAR KHAYYÁM

TOBACCO SMOKE drifts up to the dim ceiling
From a half a dozen pipes and cigarettes
Curling in endless shapes, in blue rings whirling;
As formless as our talk, Phil, drawling bets
Cornell will win the relay in a walk,
While Bob and Mac discuss the Giants' chances;
Dey in a morris-chair, Bill scowls at "Talk"
John gives large views about the last few dances.

And so it goes—an idle speech and aimless.
A few chance phrases; yet I see behind
The empty words the glow of beauty tameless
Friendship and grace and fire to strike men blind,
Till the whole world seems small and bright to hold—
Of all one's youth this hour is pure gold.

STEVEN VINCENT BENET, 1919

I BELIEVE this place is a magical place, this often haunting and often haunted place. This is a place of the "I." We're characters revealed as fate, to borrow from Heraclitus. This is the place where I learned to love this life, to curse this life and to claim this life for my very own. And as foolishly and romantic and painfully intellectual as they may seem on this beautiful spring afternoon in this most revered historic hall of learning, there is nothing in this world that I am prouder of than my ability to feel, to survive, and yes, to be a fool for what I love and believe in.

JODIE FOSTER, 1993

I COUNT MYSELF in nothing else so happy
As in a soul remembering my good friends.

WILLIAM SHAKESPEARE

A Liberal Education

Silliman College

THE THEORY of the education of that time was clearly stated in the catalogue of the College, in a passage which I will venture to quote.

"The object of the system of instruction to the undergraduates is not to give a partial education, consisting of a few branches only; nor on the other hand to give a superficial education, containing a little of almost everything; nor to finish the details of either a professional or a practical education; but to commence a thorough course, and to carry it as far as the time of the student's residence will allow. It is intended to maintain such a proportion between the different branches of literature and science, as to form a proper symmetry and balance of character. In laying the foundation of a thorough education, it is necessary that all the important faculties be brought into exercise. When certain mental endowments receive a much higher culture than others, there is a distortion in the intellectual character. The powers of the mind are not developed in their fairest proportions by studying languages alone or mathematics alone, or natural or political science alone. The object, in the proper collegiate department, is not to teach that which is peculiar to any one of the professions; but to lay the foundation which is common to them all. The principles of science and literature are the common foundation of all high intellectual attainments. They give that furniture, and discipline, and elevation to the mind, which are the best preparation for the study of a profession, or of the operations which are peculiar to the higher mercantile, manufacturing, or agricultural establishments."

TIMOTHY DWIGHT, 1903

Medical School

Yale is in many respects what Harvard used to be. It has maintained the traditions of a New England college more faithfully. Anyone visiting the two colleges would think Yale by far the older institution. The past of America makes itself felt there in many subtle ways: there is a kind of colonial self-reliance, and simplicity of aim, a touch of non-conformist separation from the great ideas and movements of the world. One is reminded, as one no longer is at Harvard, of Burke's phrase about the dissidence of dissent and the Protestantism of the Protestant religion. Nor is it only the past of America that is enshrined at Yale; the present is vividly portrayed there also. Nothing could be more American—not to say *Amurrcan*—than Yale College. The place is sacred to the national ideal. Here is sound, healthy principle, but no over scrupulousness, love of life, trust in success, a ready jocoseness, a democratic amiability, and a radiant conviction that there is nothing better than one's self. It is a boyish type of character, earnest and quick in things practical, hasty and frivolous in things intellectual. But the boyish ideal is a healthy one, and in a young man, as in a young nation, it is perfection to have only the faults of youth. There is sometimes a beautiful simplicity and completeness in the type which this ideal produces.

George Santayana, 1882

Lewie's first class was in Freshman English. Arrived at the top of Phelps Hall he saw a striking figure sitting behind the desk on the platform. It was Chauncey Brewster Tinker, aged just thirty-eight, who was teaching his first class as a full professor. He sat motionless, gazing at the top of his desk, giving his new students time to accustom themselves to his appearance: hair *en brosse*, an artificial eye, a fearful swelling on one cheek. He was dressed in a carefully pressed green suit with Homeric lapels. The last Freshman arrived and still Tinker sat without moving. Then the Chapel clock struck the half hour. He scraped back his chair, bounded to the door, slammed it shut, and began as he returned to his desk, "Shakespeare dated this play in the first speech. Did anyone notice how?" The play was *I Henry IV*, and Lewie, who had read the assignment as if his life depended upon mastering it, remembered

> *Those blessed feet*
> *Which, fourteen hundred years ago, were nail'd*
> *For our advantage, on the bitter cross,*

but he was too frightened to raise his hand. Nor did anyone else raise a hand. Tinker then quoted the passage and went on to elucidate and illuminate the text, occasionally asking a carefully prepared question, which the class soon found courage to answer caught up by the urgency of his manner and the skill of his direction. When Lewie walked down the stairs of Phelps Hall after his first class he thought, "No wonder Yale is what it is when you find such a teacher in the first class you go to." Now fifty years and more later I can still feel the excitement of Freshman English, the fear that Tink aroused, the wish to satisfy him who could be so alarming, revealing, and confidential.

Wilmarth S. Lewis, 1968

Graduate School

BREK-KE-KE-KEX coax coax
Brek-ke-ke-kex coax coax
O-op, o-op, parabalou
    Yale, Yale, Yale
Rah rah rah, rah rah rah, rah rah rah
    Team, team, team

    after ARISTOPHANES

As a privately endowed institution we must keep alive various aspects of learning which without protection run the danger of death. They may attract merely a handful of students and to the general public they may appear quite without value. Classical philology and archaeology, linguistics, Semitic languages, paleontology, aspects of the higher mathematics, and specialized scientific investigation without any apparent relation to any so-called "useful" application—these and other activities represent scholarly effort which is the University's duty to foster simply for their own sake, and because without them the heritage of human experience is impoverished.

Charles Seymour, 1939

Yale, like Ulysses, is part of all that she has met, part of all the scholars and students who have trod paths of learning across her campus, of their ideals and accomplishments, and of their lives and times, for over two and a half centuries drawing strength and inspiration and character from them all yet transcending them all in her importance to society. Such things, the environment they create and the time it takes to produce them, are irreplaceable. They must live or perish. They cannot be duplicated. They have no substitutes.

A. Whitney Griswold, 1961

Our continuing ambition is to be sure that Yale develops people, ideas and perceptions which will have a significant impact on the thought, the art, and the action of succeeding generations.

Kingman Brewster, 1965

Broadway

A LIBERAL EDUCATION is meant to instill a love of learning, and a love of the pursuit of learning, for its own sake. How also to promote a sensitive regard for the common life of others is the grand challenge. Every college devoted to encouraging the liberal education of the individual and a civilized responsibility for the rights and needs of others has therefore faced the question: how to connect how we learn and how we live? How to affiliate the intellectual pursuit of learning and the humane particularities of living?

Yale's answer to the question of how best to connect living and learning is the residential college system formally inaugurated on September 25, 1933. My conviction, stemming from experience that began upon entering a residential college precisely halfway through the fifty-year period we celebrate, is that the residential colleges, since their founding, have helped shape and focus the education of Yale undergraduates and thus provide an opportunity for combining learning and living unparalleled in this country.

A. BARTLETT GIAMATTI, 1984

BUT THE GREATEST PART of Yale then, as now, was its faculty. Maynard Mack's lectures on Shakespeare were virtuoso performances. His final lecture on Othello I will remember as long as live. There was the incomparable Henri Peyre in French literature and Charlie Fenton, swaggering, handsome Charlie Fenton, who talked out of the side of his mouth like a tough guy and whose seminar on the 20th-century novel was absolutely electric. And Professor Richard Flint in geology. A lot of us, and I was one, took geology because we had to, to fill the science requirement. And to my amazement I found out I loved it. And in every book I've written since but one, every book, geology has figured prominently in a number of ways. It stood me through much of my work and brought endless pleasure that I would never have had, and only because I was forced to do it. And best of all, the brightest star in the Yale firmament was a young instructor, a lecturer in the history of art who wasn't much older than we were. He was funny, opinionated, romantic, brilliant, never dull, never, never boring, never patronizing, irrepressibly full of life. His lectures in the history of art and architecture were standing-room-only. He threw open the windows for us, threw open the shutters, let the light in. He got us to read, got us to think, he got us to see, *to see*, and he's never stopped. When I think of the privilege of a Yale education, I think of those lectures, and to express one's admiration for such a teacher, one's abiding life-long gratitude, is probably impossible. I loved him then, I love him still, and I'm delighted he's here today. And I'm speaking of course, of Vincent Scully.

DAVID MCCULLOUGH, 1997

Woolsey Hall Auditorium

YOU HAVE COME to a great ancient university and to a College within it and an even older New England city on the water. You are not the first, nor will you be the last to come with your questions. The questions you ask yourself and will ask of Yale, and that the times will ask of you, are natural and appropriate. No one ought to approach an idea or a university in a spirit which is settled and unquestioning or smug or certain of answers or results. Intellectual curiosity, a hunger for contact with the wider world as it is aggregated here, a desire to test one's best with others, all of that is the very spirit Yale would encourage in you if Yale did not find it in you. You are in the right place.

A. BARTLETT GIAMATTI, 1980

COULD HAMLET be written by a committee, or the Mona Lisa painted by a club? Could the New Testament have been composed as a conference report? Creative ideas do not spring from groups. They spring from individuals. The divine spark leaps from the finger of God to the finger of Adam, whether it takes ultimate shape in a law of physics or a law of the land, a poem, or a policy, a sonata or a mechanical computer.

A. WHITNEY GRISWOLD, 1957

SOMETIMES some very well-meaning, perhaps cynical person is going to say to you—pretty soon in a kind of hard, knowing way: "Welcome to the real world." But you know, and you will always know because you have been educated at Yale, that Beethoven is the real world and Puccini and Gershwin are the real world, and Michelangelo and Yeats and Ella Fitzgerald and the Sermon on the Mount are the real world and Lincoln's Second Inaugural Address is the real world. Great universities are the real world; Yale University is the real world.

DAVID McCULLOUGH, 1997

AT THIS TIME of looking forward, we affirm the values of our past: to preserve and advance knowledge, to defend free inquiry and free expression, to educate leaders and thinking citizens, to teach the world around us to give scope for human achievement and to nurture human potential. We reaffirm these commitments not merely as ends in themselves, but as means to improve the human condition and elevate the human spirit.

RICHARD C. LEVIN, 1993

A LIBERAL EDUCATION is at the heart
of a civil society and the heart of a liberal
education is teaching.

Inscription, Giamatti Bench

The Spirit of Yale

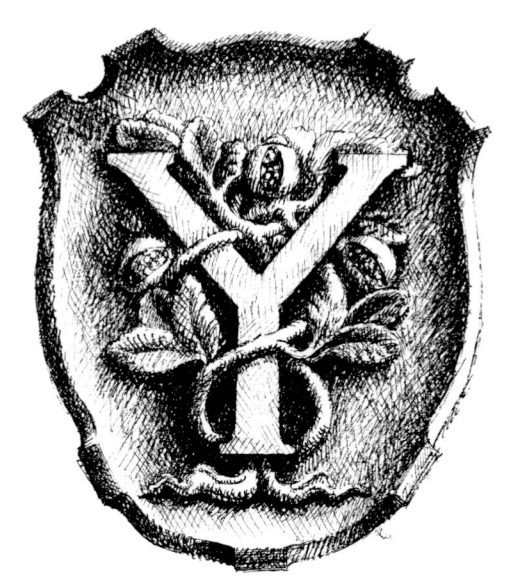

Beinecke Library

IT WAS AN EARTHLY PLACE, but strangely made
Because it slept unruffled by the cold
Immutable ironic serenade
The legal song of time, and food, and gold.

It lay beneath our common sky and yet
It was another world, a place called Yale,
A fancy land, wherein there daily met
The permanence of dust with us the frail.

We lived there once, and then across our days
Strode death, a masquerader capped and gowned,
And we, the boys whom nothing could amaze,
Stepped downward into life and so were drowned.

Quite gone—and there is only left behind
A dream of misty elms to plague the mind.

from "A Lost World"
PHELPS PUTNAM, 1916

As Freshmen First

As FRESHMEN first we came to Yale,
Fol de rol de rol rol rol
Examinations made us fail
Fol de rol de rol rol rol

Eli, Eli, Eli Yale
Fol de rol de rol rol rol
Eli, Eli, Eli Yale
Fol de rol de rol rol rol

As Sophomores we have a task
Tis best performed by torch and mask

   Chorus

In Junior year we take our ease
We smoke our pipes and sing our glees

   Chorus

In Senior year we had our parts
In making love and breaking hearts

   Chorus

And then into the world we come
We've made good friends and studied—some

   Chorus

The saddest tale we have to tell
Is when we bid old Yale farewell

   Chorus

                              Traditional

Sprague Hall

THE INSTITUTION has had a definite policy to which it has adhered with a good degree of consistency. It has employed little active agency to solicit funds. It has proposed no royal or easy paths to learning or intellectual power. It has carefully refrained from odious comparisons to the disadvantage of sister institutions. It has avoided appeals to the indolence or the undue self-reliance which are characteristic of young men. On the other hand, if the testimony of those who have known its inmost spirit and its animating forces is worth anything, it has not been too bigoted to learn nor too conceited to improve. Its windows are open in every direction, towards the rising as truly as towards the setting sun, and it is ever ready to welcome new truths from any quarter, and to try new methods, by whomsoever they are suggested, if they are recommended to our judgment or are enforced by experience. But it believes in the past as well as in the future, holding it to be eminently becoming in those who have received the torch of knowledge from those who have gone before them, to despise none of the wisdom which the past has inspired or confirmed.

W.E. DeCrow, 1884

A UNIVERSITY is not, however, a place of snobbery, though it will strike those outside the charmed circle of passwords as, at the least, remote. A university, if it is any good, is open-ended: the person of the most humble beginnings may rise to the highest office. To be sure, he is most likely to do so if he takes on something of the coloration of the university—at Yale, for example, YWAT, otherwise known as the Yale Way of Thought (the *y* pronounced as a long *e*). He must judge delicately how much of that coloration is natural to him, or he will be thought a parvenu, a climber, merely ambitious rather than incidentally ambitious. To truly enjoy such an environment, the individual—student or faculty—must harbor a well-calibrated sense of annoyance at the institution, entering into a muted adversarial relationship with YWAT, both in order to move the institution just that little bit away from what it was to what it could become, and also to assure at least the sense if not the reality of independence. The student who never misses a football game, a class, a prom, or a chance to drink a Green Cup at Mory's is not always well regarded, for a university both demands acculturation and scorns it: this is its esprit de corps. The student is told to be an individual, is then reminded of school spirit, and must, with the Greeks it is hoped he will study, find a happy moderation between independence and conformity. Only those students who assume (and make a point of disclosing their assumptions) that the anthem, code words, or way of thought at their university are inherently superior to all others are snobs, and most students and faculty accept that there are at least a few other places that, in their own peculiar way, may turn out men and women of, well, nearly the same caliber. Full professors at Harvard and Yale used to, and still generally do, receive an invitation to appear in *Who's Who in America*, simply by virtue of that achievement; they know that this "honor," like so many honors, is an act of theater, and while they may take delight in ceremony, in gowns and hoods, in addressing each other in faculty meetings as Mr. President, or Mr. Dean, they are not so pompous as they sound. They understand the nurturing value of tradition while knowing that some of that tradition has little purpose beyond being fun. In such an environment one might reasonably expect to find a number of people, students, faculty, alumni, and staff, who have a wide-ranging curiosity, a somewhat childlike desire to collect experiences and to see places, to know because knowing itself is fun.

ROBIN WINKS, 1987

Linonia & Brothers Library

THERE IS IN THIS ANCIENT PLACE a powerful surge to connectedness, or at least to collectivity. Founded by Congregationalists, Yale has always been marked by an instinct for groups, assemblages, aggregations. The place effortlessly generates congregations, and—Yale has been, and I trust forever will be, hospitable to the entrepreneur of the mind, the solitary genius, the happy loner—the intellectual and social landscape is dotted with collectivities and sodalities, small bands and teams and caucuses and alliances and societies and committees and gaggles and clutches, their size never fixed but ideally not varying much between a dozen and a dozen and a half, such a span embracing most singing groups, theatrical troupes, publication staffs, much of an entryway, many joint research efforts, senior societies, almost all seminars, large number of clubs and organizations, and the Yale Corporation.

A. BARTLETT GIAMATTI, 1986

Mother of Men

Mother of Men, grown strong in giving,
Honor to them thy lights have led;
Rich in the toil of thousands living
Proud of the deeds of thousands dead.
We who have felt thy pow'r and known thee,
We in whose work thy gifts avail,
High in our hearts enshrined, enthrone thee,
Mother of Men, Old Yale.

Spirit of Youth, alive, unchanging,
Under whose feet the years are cast
Heir to an ageless empire, ranging
Over the future and the past;
Thee, whom our fathers loved before us,
Thee, whom our sons unborn shall hail.
Praise we to-day in sturdy chorus,
Mother of Men, Old Yale.

Brian Hooker
Seth Bingham

Of course, there had long been a tradition at Yale of the bright, hard-working outsider who emerged as a class leader and may have even saved the Harvard game in the final seconds. The man elected captain of the football team in Owen Johnson's *Stover at Yale* was not Dink Stover, one of the fictional Yale heroes Pudge had referred to at Denny's memorial, but the greatly respected Tom Regan, who described himself as having "come from nothing." Stover himself would not have qualified as an outsider by the brown shoe standards of the fifties. His name was already known at Yale when he arrived from Lawrenceville, where he had been captain of the football team and vice president of the school—although he had attained those positions, the reader is told, after having fought his way up from "a ridiculous beginning." By the time we arrived at Yale, the appearance of the bright outsider was no longer accidental. There was a broad and conscious movement into the white middle class and toward the West, a sort of *apertura* to the yahoos. The alternative to Yale's broadening its base to become a truly national institution was later stated in a blunt piece of hyperbole by Kingman Brewster, who was the president of Yale during an acceleration of the transition a decade or so after Denny and I had left: "I do not intend to preside over a finishing school on Long Island Sound."

Calvin Trillin, 1993

ANND WHENN reunion's day is past,
And Memory's lamp obscuring,
The wassail cup of friendship true
Will linger, time enduring

In requiem Harkness chimes will sing
Elysian fields will beckon
Then is when you'll cross the bar,
The Great Beyond to reckon

Saint Peter will cast a knowing wink
When you come into sight
"Welcome to heaven, old Blue," he'll say,
"The Yale Club's to the right."

JULIEN DEDMAN, 1950

ON WEDNESDAY MORNING the commemoration exercises, the major event of the celebration, took place. Since the bicentennial auditorium, Woolsey Hall, was not finished, the ceremonies were held in the Hyperion Theater. There Justice Brewer (B.A. 1856) of the United States Supreme Court gave the commemorative address on Yale in its relation to public service, and then honorary degrees were given to sixty-two worthies including Mark Twain and Theodore Roosevelt. Roosevelt, the only recipient to speak, said of Yale what it most liked to hear: "I have never yet worked at a task worth doing that I did not find myself working shoulder to shoulder with some son of Yale. I have never yet been in any struggle for righteousness or decency, that there were not men of Yale to aid me and give me strength and courage."

BROOKS KELLEY, 1974

Art School Bridge

BETWEEN the national leadership enjoyed by Yale's graduates and the strenuousness of its undergraduate life, the vigor of its social code, the distinction and earnestness of its faculty, and the broad discipline of its course of instruction there has always been an intimate connection. And Yale still believes in character and fair play, in learning and teaching the truth. It remains, as it has always been, a nursery of scholars and a gateway to that life whose test is achievement and public service.

GEORGE W. PIERSON, 1967

Mory's

Whiffenpoof Song

TO THE TABLES down at Mory's
To the place where Louis dwells,
To the dear old Temple Bar we love so well.
Sing the Whiffenpoofs assembled,
With their glasses raised on high,
And the magic of their singing casts a spell.
Yes the magic of their singing
Of the songs we love so well,
Shall I Wasting, and Mavourneen, and the rest.
We will serenade our Louis
While life and voice shall last,
Then we'll pass and be forgotten, with the rest.

We are poor little lambs, who have lost our way.
Baa Baa Baa.
We are little black sheep who have gone astray.
Baa Baa Baa.
Gentlemen songsters off on a spree,
Damned from here to eternity.
God have mercy on such as we.
Baa Baa Baa.

MEADE MINNIGERODE
GEORGE S. POMEROY, 1910

Bulldog

BULLDOG, bulldog, bow wow wow,
Eli Yale.
Bulldog, bulldog, bow wow wow,
Our team can never fail
When the sons of Eli break through the line
That is the sign we hail!
Bulldog, bulldog, bow wow wow,
Eli Yale!

COLE PORTER, 1911

Down the Field

MARCH, march on down the field
Fighting for Eli
Break through that crimson line,
Their strength to defy;
We'll give a long cheer for Eli's men
We're here to win again
Harvard's team may fight to the end,
But Yale will win!

C. W. O'CONNER
STANLEIGH P. FRIEDMAN, 1904

Presentation Day, 1869

THEIR SONGS are done, their forms are gone,
    And Time for us hath turned the glass:
We heed not, as we take their seats,
    How downward swift the red sands pass.

We heed not how the cloud comes on
    That shadows all the sunny land—
The day when heart from heart must part
    And clinging hand unlink from hand.

What shall the Dies Irae give
    In place of that it takes away:
How fill the time we have to live
    While youth treads downward to decay?

Good-by, true friend; good-by, old Yale;
    Good-by, each dear familiar spot;
Good-by, sweet season of our youth—
    "The golden, happy, unforgot."

HENRY A. BEERS

Woolsey Hall Rotunda

OH YOUTH forgone, forgoing!
Oh dreams unseen, unsought!
God give you joy of knowing
What light your death has brought.

Inscription, Woolsey Hall Rotunda

WATCHING THE SUN GO DOWN . . . at the end of the Day of the Hundredth Game, the sensitive observer could not help but feel moved. The Game has had a long and robust life, flourishing in all kinds of political and economic climates, surviving wars and depressions and the more insidious mildew of ever-changing tastes and fashions. Though it is, to be sure, on the face of it, a family affair, it is also a national heritage and its kingdom is vaster than it might seem at first sight. Without the example of the Crimson and the Blue, loyally supported by the Tiger of old Nassau—institutions which a hundred years ago were uniquely privileged in manpower, prestige and athletic elan vital—it is difficult to see how the sport would have flourished as it has throughout the country. Without the example of the early pioneers there would be no Superbowl. But more important, the Game has been, for a century now, played invariably with dedication and good sportsmanship by youngsters who are student-athletes, with emphasis on the first element. And in its hundredth birthday it is still in the prime of life.

THOMAS G. BERGIN, 1984

IN THE SIX MONTHS between being named president of Yale University in December of 1977 and taking office in July of 1978, I had ample opportunity to receive advice. . . .

I, of course, had no policies. I had a mortgage and one suit but no policies. I cast about. . . . What was it Yale needed most, wanted most, and that would most contribute to solving our deficit, enhancing our quality, and making me a Manager.

One night in early April, 1978, crouched in my garage, as I was trying to memorize the Trustee's names, particularly the ones I had met, it came to me, and I wrote right there between the lawnmower and the snow tires a memo. On July 1, 1978 I issued this memo to an absent and indifferent University. It read:

In order to repair what Milton called the ruin of our grandparents, I wish to announce that henceforth, as a matter of University policy, evil is abolished and paradise is restored.

I trust all of you will do whatever possible to achieve this policy objective.

A. BARTLETT GIAMATTI, 1989

WHEN WE CAME to break up housekeeping at the end of Senior year, we found the process a simple one, . . . I remember my last night in the dismantled room, where the slanting bedstead and debilitated chairs stood about confusedly on the bare floor. It was the evening of Presentation Day. The class histories had been read, the ivy planted, the parting ode sung. The class had marched around with the band, cheering each of the old buildings in turn, and had then broken ranks forever. I had taken supper with my chum, and bidden him good-by at the station, being about to leave myself on the following morning. The entry was quite deserted when I climbed the staircase to our room. I had no lamp, so I lit a cigar, and, sitting down in the dark, by the open window, listened to the din of the summer insects and the rustle of the breeze in the elms. The crowd of the afternoon had dispersed, and the yard was quite still. Most of the underclassmen had gone away some days before, and only a few lights glimmered along the college row. At the formal leave-taking in Alumni Hall, where many of the fellows had been "all broke up," I had felt no emotion; and my chum and myself had agreed, in talking it over at supper, that the ceremony was not in good taste. One is always apt to resent a set of occasions for grief and to refuse to honor any such draft on the feelings, just as one takes a perverse pleasure in declining to be impressed to order by a famous landscape or picture or cathedral. The soul must take its own time. But now, as I sat alone in the deserted room and realized that pleasant chapter of life was closed, that youth was over and friends were gone, and that I must put forth on the morrow from the green shelter of Alma Mater, I discovered that I had struck deeper roots in the life of the last four years than I had even suspected.

HENRY A. BEERS, 1910

Sterling Library and Cross Campus

"YOU'RE PRETTY FINE, Joe," said Brockhurst to their surprise. "Well, it's good enough as it is. It takes an awful lot to stir it, but it's the most sensitive of the American colleges, and it will respond. It wants to do the right thing. Some day I'll see it. I'm a crank, of course." He stopped, and Stover felt in his voice a little note of bitterness. "The trouble with me is just that. I'm impractical; have strange ideas. I'm not satisfied with Yale as a magnificent factory on democratic business lines; I dream of something else, something visionary, a great institution not of boys, clean lovable and honest, but of men or brains, of courage, of leadership, a great center of thought, to stir the country and bring it back to the understanding of what man creates with his imagination, and dares with his will. It's visionary—it will come."

OWEN JOHNSON, 1912

Bright College Years

Bᴙɪɢʜᴛ ᴄᴏʟʟᴇɢᴇ ʏᴇᴀʀs, with pleasure rife,
The shortest, gladdest years of life;
How swiftly are ye gliding by,
Oh, why doth time so quickly fly!
The seasons come, the seasons go,
The earth is green, or white with snow;
But time and change shall naught avail
To break the friendships formed at Yale.

In after-years, should troubles rise
To cloud the blue of sunny skies,
How bright will seem, through memory's haze,
Those happy, golden, bygone days!
Oh, let us strive that ever we
May let these words our watch-cry be,
Where'er upon life's sea we sail:
"For God, for Country, and for Yale."

H. S. Dᴜʀᴀɴᴅ
Cᴀʀʟ Wɪʟʜᴇʟᴍ

Index

Aristophanes, 82
Art School Bridge, 99
"As Freshmen First," 92

Baldwin, H., 27
Beers, Henry A., Professor
    The Memorial Quadrangle, 30, 43, 49, 55
    The Ways of Yale, 30, 49, 59, 102, 105
Beinecke Library, 90
Beinecke Plaza, 34
Benet, Steven Vincent, 75
Bergin, Thomas G., Professor, 104
    The Game
Berkeley College, 58
Bingham, Hiram, 23
    Elihu Yale
Bingham, Seth, 96
"Bingo," 73
"Blue Roses of Academus," 49
Boathouse at Derby, 69
"Boola," 61
Branford College, 40
"Brave Mother Yale," 47
Brewster, Kingman, President of the University, 1963–1977, 83
    Remembrances
"Bright College Years," 107
Bronson, Frederick W., 31, 56, 61
    The Editor's Window
Broadway, 84
"Bulldog," 101
Burton, Martha, 68
    1982 Yale Banner

Calhoun College, 53
Camp, Walter, 51, 52
    Yale, Her Campus, Classrooms and Athletics
Chapel Street, 15
Connecticut Hall, 44

"Consule Planco," 43
Cross Campus, 106
Cross, Wilbur L., Dean
    A Connecticut Yankee, 50
    Thanksgiving Proclamation, 29

Davenport College, 17
DeCrow, W. E., 53, 93
    Yale and the City of Elms
Dedman, Julien, 98
    Boola Boola
Dexter, Franklin Bowditch, 19, 20
    A Documentary History of Yale University
Divinity School, 14
DeVane, William Clyde, Dean, 12
Dodge, H. G., 71
Douglas, William, 36
"Down the Field," 101
Dummer, Jeremiah, 20, 22
Durand, H. S., 107
Durfee Hall, 66
Dwight, Timothy, President of the University, 1886–1899, 15, 79
    Memories of Yale Life and Men

East Rock, 28
Eli Book, 54

Foster, Jodie, 75
    1993 Yale Banner
French, Robert Dudley, Professor, 16, 17, 18, 19, 20, 22, 28, 33, 37, 39, 44
    The Memorial Quadrangle
Friedman, Stanleigh P., 71, 101

"Gaudeamus," 65
Giamatti, A. Bartlett, President of the University, 1978–1986
    1986 Baccalaureate Address, 95
    1980 Freshman Address, 86

[Giamatti, A. Bartlett]
   1984 Yale Banner, 84
   Yale Alumni Magazine, December
      1989, 104
Graduate School, 82
Griswold, A. Whitney, President of the
      University, 1951–1963, 83, 87
   Yale, A History
"Goodnight Poor Harvard," 70

Hansen, Keith, 72
   1982 Yale Banner
Harkness Tower, 42
Havemeyer, Loomis, 48
   Out of Yale's Past
Hillhouse Avenue, 35
Hirsch, Allan M., 61
Hooker, Brian, 96
Housman, A. E., 67
   The Collected Poems of A. E. Housman

Ingalls Rink, 60
Ivy Ode, 59

Jonathan Edwards College, 38
Johnson, Owen, 11, 106
   Stover at Yale

Kelley, Brooks M., 98
   Yale, A History
Kelly, Tina, 34
   1983 Yale Banner
Khayyam, Omar, 74
   The Rubaiyat of Omar Khayyam
Kiesling, Stephen, 69
   The Catch
Kline Biology Tower, 60
Knickerbocker, The, 35

Law School, 56
Laws of Yale College, 45
Levin, Richard C., President of the
      University, 1993–   , 9, 87
Lewis, Wilmarth S., 57, 81
   One Man's Education
Linonia and Brothers Library, 95
Lorimer, Linda Koch, 9
"Lost World, A," 91

MacLeish, Archibald, 39
Mather, Cotton, 21
May, Georges, Dean, 58
McCullough, David, 85, 87
   1997 Yale Banner
Medical School, 80
Merrill, Charles Edmund, 47
Minnigerode, Meade, 100
Moore, Douglas S., 70
Moore, Paul, 32
   My Harvard, My Yale
Morse College, 47
Mory's, 100
"Mother of Men," 96

"'Neath the Elms," 27
New Haven Green, 31
"New Yale, The," 55

O'Connor, C. W., 101
Osborn Laboratory, 60

Payne Whitney Gymnasium, 64
Phelps Gateway, 10
Pierson College, 26
Pierson, George W., Professor, 62, 99
Pomeroy, George S., 100
Porter, Cole, 73, 101
"Presentation Day, 1869," 102
Putnam, Phelps, 91

Roosevelt, Franklin D., 73

Santayana, George, 80
   Yale, A History
Saybrook College, 23
Schiff, Judith Ann, 38
Science Hill, 60
Seymour, Charles, President of the
      University, 1937–1951, 83
   Yale, A History
Shakespeare, William, 76
Sheffield Sterling Strathcona Hall, 37
Shepard, Thomas G., 47
Silliman College, 78
Sprague Hall, 93
Sterling Library, 24, 106
Stiles College, 47
Student Room, 72

Thompson, George E., 52
The Quiet House
Timothy Dwight College, 33
Trillin, Calvin, 97
Remembering Denny
Trumbull College, 71

University Commons, 68

"Wake, Freshmen Wake," 66
"When I Was One and Twenty," 67
"Whiffenpoof Song," 100
White, Milton, 74
A Yale Man

Woolsey Hall, 55
Woolsey Hall Auditorium, 86
Woolsey Hall Rotunda, 103
"Whoop It Up," 71
Wilhelm, Carl, 107
Winks, Robin, Professor, 94
Cloak and Gown
Wood, John Seymour, 46, 67
College Days
Wright Hall, 66

Yale Bowl, 70
Yale, Elihu, 23